MADRID CHIC

PHOTOGRAPHY BY OLIVER PILCHER
TEXT BY CRISTINA CARRILLO DE ALBORNOZ

MADRID CHIC

ASSOULINE

Introduction

Freedom is the perfume that is breathed in the streets of Madrid. It is a magic word that Madrilenians understand very well.

— Mario Vargas Llosa, Nobel Prize Laureate in Literature

The soul of Eternal Rome lies in its timeless beauty, while Paris, the marvelously refined grande dame that has earned the name "City of Love," oozes romance. And Madrid? Oh, Madrid's heart! Strong, vibrant, warm, joyful, and inspiring, it seduces from the moment you set foot in the city. If life were a city, it would be Madrid. One can live so many lives in the same day in Madrid that the desire to live intensely becomes contagious.

"How good your name sounds, breakwater of all Spain!" wrote Antonio Machado, one of Spain's greatest twentieth-century poets, complimenting the Spanish capital that, regardless of the circumstances, "always smiles." An authentic blend of all the regions of Spain—indeed, the sum of them all—Madrid is "the cheerful engine" of the country.

Painter Sandra Rojo and her husband Gabriel Suárez, founder of "Lucha de Gigantes," walking near Villa Rosa, a traditional tavern turned into a *tablao*, a place where flamenco shows are performed. *Previous pages:* Commissioned by King Philip IV in 1629, the Buen Retiro Palace served as a second home for Spain's royal families for more than 200 years. Remains of the palace are on view in Retiro Park.

What really makes Madrid's spirit special is its passionate, friendly people. Madrilenians are so open that when you go out with a group of friends, you end up dancing with an entire bar. No one feels alone in Madrid. The proximity of the people makes everyone feel at home. One of the most wonderful things about Madrid is that it's everyone's city. It does not ask anyone where they come from or where they are going. Madrid is a city of settlers—people who come to Madrid, people who choose Madrid, and anyone who settles in Madrid becomes a Madrilenian forever.

There is a popular saying about the Spanish capital: "From Madrid to heaven," meaning that once you see and experience Madrid, heaven is the next best thing. Apparently, the phrase became famous at the end of the eighteenth century as a result of the architectural and urban reforms that King Charles III, known as *el mejor alcalde de Madrid* ("Madrid's best mayor"), carried out to embellish and modernize the city. Thanks to his vision, Madrid stopped being an old-fashioned Castilian town and was transformed into a royal capital of a vast empire. In addition to completing the Royal Palace and the Botanic Gardens and starting work on the Prado Museum, Charles III was one of Madrid's greatest architects, commissioning many of its monumental landmarks, such as the Cibeles and Neptuno fountains and the neoclassical Puerta de Alcalá gate. In a similar vein, the current mayor, José Luis Martínez-Almeida, is one of the driving forces behind Madrid's success today. It is a city that has captured the world's attention, where everyone wants to go, and that has given a new twist to the old saying: "From heaven to Madrid," meaning that one can only improve on heaven by going to Madrid.

Previous pages: (left) French-style gardens at Palacio Liria, the official residence of the Duke of Alba, head of the House of Alba. Built in the eighteenth century, Liria Palace houses one of the foremost art collections in the world. It opened its doors to the public in 2019. (*right*) Fernando Fitz-James Stuart and Sofía Palazuelo, the 17th Duke and Duchess of Huéscar, walking in the gardens of Liria Palace. The Duke of Huéscar — together with his brother Carlos, Count of Osorno—supported the policies, introduced by their father, the Duke of Alba, of opening their palaces and sharing the Casa de Alba legacy with the citizens of Madrid.
Following pages: (left) The entrance gallery, or "Winter Garden," of interior designer Lorenzo Castillo's home. This eighteenth-century palace, built by the then king's architect, Ventura Rodriguez, was rehabilitated by Castillo. The walls are upholstered with emerald fabrics that he designed himself, and there is furniture by Renzo Mongiardino. (*right*) Lorenzo Castillo, in the main salon of his home, seated next to a screen by Aldo Tura, on a sofa of his own design. The luxurious green armchairs once belonged to the Dukes of Windsor.

Madrid, one of Europe's most historically rich cities, is inextricably tied to centuries of court life. To understand the lively, complex spirit of Madrid is to take to heart the unique merging of its extraordinary cultural and artistic heritage—traditions cultivated over thousands of years—and its modern eagerness to be part of the vanguard and innovation.

The city's documented history can be traced back to the ninth century, when the Umayyad emir of Córdoba, Muhammad I, founded the city, naming it Mayrit. The city flourished during the Arab occupation of the Iberian Peninsula, but later fell into Christian hands during the Reconquista of Spain. In 1083, King Alfonso VI recognized Madrid's strategic potential and took over the city. Then, in 1561, King Philip II moved the court to Madrid; although he made no official declaration, the seat of the court became the de facto capital. King Philip ruled the Spanish empire, inherited from his father, at its peak, when it spanned all five known continents. He was a monarch of vast culture, a refined, cosmopolitan man akin to a Renaissance Italian prince. A grand patron of the arts, he was Titian's most important benefactor, bought most of Hieronymus Bosch's oeuvre, ate on Ming dinner plates from silver dishes, and collected the most outstanding and exotic cabinet of curiosities. Most importantly, he conceived El Escorial—the ultimate architectural triumph of the Spanish Renaissance. Its monumental yet severely sober style epitomizes the splendor that the city of Madrid inherited. The king's legacy, furthermore, is mirrored in the timeless elegant spirit of Madrid and the dignified bearing of Madrilenians.

During the seventeenth century, Madrid grew rapidly. The royal court attracted Spain's leading artists and writers in this *siglo de oro* ("golden century") of culture, including Miguel de Cervantes, author of *Don Quixote,* and master painter Diego Velázquez. The neighborhood where the writers lived still bears the evocative name *el Barrio de las Letras* (the Literary Quarter), its

streets the setting of many novels. Although the whole area has undergone a major redevelopment, Madrid remains a strongly literary city, which has served as the backdrop for celebrated works from Cervantes to Benito Pérez Galdós, and from García Lorca to Ernest Hemingway. "This city overflows with literature, poetry, and music on all four sides, so much so that it is itself a literary character," wrote the Spanish-Peruvian Mario Vargas Llosa, recipient of the Nobel Prize in Literature. He himself began to write the first version of his novel *La ciudad y los perros* (published as *The Time of the Hero* in English) in a Madrid coffee shop, a work that made him one of the best-known Latin American authors in the world.

It was under King Charles III (1716–1788) that Madrid became a truly modern city, and his reforms encouraged European travelers to visit. During the Romantic movement, the allure of the city was particularly strong among English and French Romantics, who were captivated by its beloved past, its customs, and its exoticism. From that point on, fascination with the country, especially Andalusia and Madrid, continued to grow into the twentieth century.

The 1980s were a major turning point for the city, when the exuberant countercultural movement La Movida Madrileña ("The Madrid Scene") ushered in a new sense of freedom and creativity during the Spanish transition to democracy. Film director Pedro Almodóvar, pop singer Alaska, writer Francisco Umbral, and photographer Ouka Leele were among the many creatives to make their mark on Spanish and world culture. Art dealers such as the Viscount of Torre Hidalgo, director of Magna Art Auctions, remembers how they used to say they were "the new Picassos."

However, only in recent times has this southern capital of Europe become the captivating *place to be,* attracting people from all corners of the world. "Madrid has gone from being the best-kept secret to a revelation city," Mayor Martínez-Almeida tells me on the top floor of Cibeles Palace, the town hall headquarters. During his honeymoon this year, in remote areas of Bhutan and the Maldives, the drivers of his motorcycle taxis were carrying Real Madrid flags and scarves. Only ten years ago, people outside Europe would talk about Barcelona or Seville when referring to Spain, rarely mentioning Madrid; in a way, there was a complete lack of knowledge of the city. Thus, the lovely anecdote from far away reassured the mayor, once again, that the perception of the city abroad had been totally transformed. Madrid is now among the great capitals of the world; "it definitely has a good flow," or, as the locals say, *buen rollo,* and people just love to go with it.

If Bhutan has its Gross National Happiness Index, woven into its constitution as a measure of success, in Madrid the index would measure its joy. Maybe, as the mayor suggests, the height of cool today is that one can go from the Prado, one of the most important museums in the world, to a Taylor Swift or Bruce Springsteen concert in the recently renovated Santiago Bernabéu Stadium, often referred to as the "modern Colosseum" and home of the Real Madrid soccer team. Real Madrid, recognized by FIFA as the best sports club of the twentieth century—a titan atop the list of all-time Champions League winners—is without doubt a magnificent world ambassador for Spain, but Madrid is its home, and the city couldn't be prouder.

Although Madrid was hit hard by the 2008 financial crisis, a turning point for the city occurred during the challenging times of the Covid-19 pandemic, when its lifestyle was tested. At a certain point after the first wave of the pandemic, when all the cities remained locked down, Isabel Díaz Ayuso, president of the

Following pages: (left) Rafael Medina: 20th Duke of Feria, 17th Marquis of Villalba and Spanish Grandee, gentleman, entrepreneur and sportsman. He recently launched MR. AB, a new lifestyle brand with a storefront at Galería Canalejas. Medina is photographed on the rooftop terrace of the Four Seasons hotel in Madrid. *(right)* The Telefónica Building, inaugurated in 1930 as part of the project for the Gran Vía, was built by architect Ignacio de Cárdenas Pastor. At one point it was the first skyscraper in Europe for its height of almost 90 meters.

region, made the decision to open Madrid gradually. And with it, Díaz Ayuso—a confident, strong woman who is constantly infusing a tremendous energy into the city—surprised the world by maintaining the essence of Madrid's lifestyle: its spirit of freedom. After consulting epidemiologists, she began to open restaurants, theaters, hotels (hence her nickname "Queen of Hoteliers")…and the world turned its eyes on Madrid, asking, "What kind of city is that where everything is open?" It acted like a magnet. Together with Mayor Martínez-Almeida, both political forces guided by liberal policies, Díaz Ayuso succeeded in boosting the local economy, raising the city's profile internationally, and helping attract foreign investment. Along the way, many Latin Americans who had settled in Miami decided to move to Madrid instead. Spain, the house of *la Hispanidad* (Spanish heritage) in Europe, with historical and cultural ties dating back centuries, was perhaps their natural destiny after all.

Fashion designer Roberto Torretta, who was born in Argentina and has lived in Spain since 1972, recalls that Madrid was a kind of black-and-white city when he first arrived. Then, in the '80s, it became Technicolor. And what about now? "The timing is just right, a magic moment where all seems to be aligned, like a CinemaScope city." Torretta married Carmen Echevarria, a pivotal fashion figure, and they, along with the likes of the brilliant design house Sybilla—regarded as Balenciaga's heir—and Loewe, with its revolutionary shop windows, marked a new era in Madrid fashion: the arrival of postmodernity. Loewe, the Spanish luxury house founded in 1846 in Madrid as a small leather-goods maker, and acquired in 1996 by LVMH, has become stratospherically popular recently; Rihanna performed at the Super Bowl halftime show in 2023 dressed in Loewe, and superstar Zendaya almost broke the fashion internet with a look by Loewe in 2024.

Following pages: The stage is set at Las Ventas, one of the most important bullrings in the world.

In the last five years, Madrid, more alive and creative than ever, has been reinvigorated from top to bottom. Elite luxury hotels have opened, and palatial old ones, such as the Mandarin Oriental Ritz, the Westin Palace Madrid, and Santo Mauro, have undergone extended renovations. The city has become a mecca for world cuisine and cutting-edge interior design. The Teatro Real enjoys unique international prestige, while the best orchestras and musicians decide to open their Southern European tours in Madrid.

Urban conditions have improved tremendously, with bohemian areas such as Las Salesas turning into the coolest districts, and "dull" neighborhoods, such as the one next to the Manzanares riverbank, becoming fashionable again, recalling life in Madrid as captured by Goya in masterworks such as his *Meadow of San Isidro*. The Royal Collections Gallery (Galería de las Colecciones Reales), tracing five hundred years of history and the biggest museum project of our times, recently opened. The contemporary art scene is richer than ever as new art galleries, such as Opera, and art auction houses, like Magna Art Auctions, flow into the city. Right behind Antonio López, the most important living Spanish artist and painter of Madrid landscapes, stand masters like Manolo Valdés, Cristina Iglesias, Jaume Plensa, and Arturo Berned, the latter making his mark on the new Parque Norte with his inspiring monumental sculptures.

Pascua Ortega, the czar of Spanish interior design, who just received the Award for International Excellence for his extraordinary legacy of elevating the aesthetics of modernity, exclaims, "Every city has its momentum, the best of times, and now it's Madrid experiencing a stellar, fascinating time." The maestro is uttering these words while making a toast to the city during one of his celebrated lunches, this time in honor of this book. As usual, there are refined floral arrangements by Inés Urquijo, whose work

is sought after from the Hamptons to the South of France. As if composing a symphony, the interior designer has gathered twenty-five guests—the crème de la crème of Madrid's society—in his house, a nineteenth-century palace in the Las Letras neighborhood that belonged to a minister of Queen Isabella II, its exquisite inner garden patio presided over by a lemon tree. Ortega knows what he's talking about: his great-grandfather, prominent Spanish historian/politician Joaquín Costa, was the leading figure in the intellectual movement known as "regenerationism," aimed at forging a new identity for late-nineteenth-century and early-twentieth-century Spain following decades of stagnation. Indeed, Madrid is an alluvial city that's reinvented day by day.

Nonetheless, what's paramount, beyond Madrid's ability to transform itself into a cosmopolitan capital, is that the city has been able to keep its imprint. Modern Madrid fascinates so powerfully because it has not lost a bit of its essence. The skyline, for example, retains its distinctive character. Essentially flat, it charms with its paucity of tall buildings (among them the Four Skyscrapers towers, in a new business area announcing the city's expansion toward the north). We can feel the city's monumentality and architectural weight, reinforced by its many sculptures with historical significance atop rooftops, such as Minerva on the Metrópolis and the two marvelous bronze chariots sculpted by Higinio de Basterra, ridden by two charioteers, crowning the former headquarters of the Bank of Bilbao and the current building of the Ministry of Environment.

Old and new Madrid coexist so wonderfully that they enrich each other, a fact that has inspired leading architects around the world, from Zaha Hadid to Santiago Calatrava, to create modern landmarks here, giving new life to the best historic buildings. The French Pritzker Prize winner Jean Nouvel designed

King Juan Carlos I with Esther Koplowitz, Marchioness of Cárdenas, at the Royal Academy of History, where she was honored with the Golden Medal. In 2023, the Royal Academy of Medicine awarded her the Medal of Honor for her contributions to medicine and biomedical research, activities which she promotes as the President of the Esther Koplowitz Foundation, which is focused on improving the quality of life for those in need. A great philanthropist and a remarkable businesswoman, she is also the Vice President of the FCC Group.

the expansion of the Reina Sofía National Museum, raising the status of the historic stone hospital and creating a plaza between the two buildings that is a kind of protected neighborhood. Swiss firm Herzog & de Meuron converted an 1899 power plant into the CaixaForum art center, a new architectural point of interest that rises over old Madrid. Rafael Moneo was in charge of the first expansion of the Prado Museum, and Norman Foster, who oversaw the second one, went on to open his own Norman Foster Foundation in the city, connecting architecture, design, and arts to better serve society.

Elena Ochoa, the famed architect's wife, is CEO and founder of Ivorypress, a Madrid publishing house specializing in art books. "Madrid is a provincial city by nature, and that is where its charm lies," says Lady Foster, expanding on the unique spirit of the city. "And it remains a deeply provincial, human city despite its cosmopolitanism. The global Madrid of these years continues to be intrinsically local. It is encouraging to note that when you walk through the different districts, their DNA has not changed."

Madrid is an incredible walking city, its neighborhoods full of contrasts, each with its own charm and different flavor. Sundays in Madrid mean one thing: going to El Rastro flea market, which is also an important social gathering place for Madrilenians. There is something idiosyncratic about Madrid residents—their fondness for their neighborhood, and their curiosity to explore others.

It is a tradition proudly transmitted from parents to children, as warmly remembered by Sara Aznar, the Spanish-Uruguayan owner of trendy restaurant Los 33, who settled with her family in the fashionable boho-chic neighborhood of Las Salesas. With its European air and touch of traditionalism, Las Salesas is one of the most interesting areas in the city, a place Sara affectionately calls the "Sojo of Madrid," the "j" instead of the "h" a wink at Spanish ham.

To that end, a meaningful lesson drawn from the "new Madrid" is that Madrilenians are finally proud to show the world what's happening in their city, as opposed to what happened before, when "good" was defined by what came from outside. This enthusiastic feeling is shared by many, observes Elisabeth Horcher, a member of the fourth generation to run the legendary eighty-year-old restaurant Horcher. Over lunch—a venison carpaccio with mustard seeds and spicy figs—she tells me that what has happened in Madrid over the last five years is a wonderful madness, and she is truly proud to be part of it. "At last, we believe in our traditions, our fantastic cultural heritage and its potential. This makes us all feel humble, staying true to our roots," she says.

Since the 1940s, Horcher has been a unique witness to the history of Madrid, attracting regulars like Dalí, Hemingway, Sophia Loren, John Wayne, Baroness Thyssen-Bornemisza, the Duke of Alba, and the King of Spain, who are drawn to its elegant yet friendly service, old-world cuisine, and classic decor. The tables are decorated with small bouquets of carnations in silver pots—the carnation has been a symbol of Spain, and of Madrid, since the sixteenth century. During the annual San Isidro festivities in May, carnations are everywhere, in the buttonholes of *isidros*' jackets or woven into *isidras*' hair.

Even more beautiful is how the carnation became a Spanish symbol: On his honeymoon in Granada in 1526, Holy Roman Emperor Charles V, who was also King of Spain at the time, decided to give his wife flowers as a symbol of his eternal love—not just any flowers but carnations, which were not cultivated in Europe and had to be brought in from Persia. How appropriate that this chic—or, more precisely, elegant—tradition is rooted in the deep past.

Previous pages: Manicured gardens—with French, Italian, and Spanish influences—seen from the pavilion of a private collector's residence. In the distance, there is a totem sculpture by Ellsworth Kelly. *Following pages: (left)* Jantaminiau Couture Fall/Winter 2011 dress worn by a character in the film *The Hunger Games: Catching Fire. (right)* Dutch couturier Jan Taminiau and his husband Juan Várez's apartment/atelier on Calle Lagasca 90. Among Taminiau's devotees are Queen Máxima of the Netherlands, Beyoncé, and Lady Gaga.

Finally, looking back is cool, and this is how Nino Redruello, Madrid's passionate chef, gastro agitator, and fourth-generation owner of La Ancha restaurant, has won fame with his rooftop restaurant Club Financiero Génova in the Colón Center. Faithful to his family's 104 years as restaurateurs, Redruello sees his calling as "a return to the ancestral," with iconic dishes like *tortilla velazqueña* with tripe (a wink to the painter Velázquez). Redruello remains unpretentious, thrilled by a major shift over the last few years in the social standing of chefs, whose profession had previously been considered somewhat lowly and is now a prestigious métier.

That is how Madrid started on its journey to become a mecca of gastronomy—offering everything from venerable to groundbreaking dining experiences, from Sobrino de Botín, the world's oldest restaurant, founded in 1725 (and location for the final scene of Hemingway's 1926 novel *The Sun Also Rises*), to DiverXO, the fourth-best restaurant in the world, helmed by David Muñoz, the most transgressive of avant-garde Spanish chefs. Not to mention the genuinely authentic food markets, from El Mercado de la Paz to Mercado de Maravillas, equally places for spectacle, full of natural light and tapas bars, and acquiring the best local products at La Duquesita artisan pastry shop and Mantequerías Bravo, a gourmet icon that has been in the same family since its founding in 1931.

Madrid cuisine has been evolving at the speed of a rocket. Or, with the city hosting a Formula One Grand Prix in 2026, we could perhaps more appropriately say Madrid has become the leader on the racetrack. This is the vision of seven-Michelin-star chef Quique Dacosta, who has transformed the renovated Mandarin Oriental Ritz into the most exciting culinary destination in Madrid. The iconic hotel's five culinary spaces—three restaurants (Deessa, Palm Court, and the Ritz Garden) and two new bars (Pictura and Champagne

Bar)—have all been created and managed by him. Deessa, with two Michelin stars, is the most unique of the five, embodying the elegant, palatial spirit of the Ritz. Entering the hotel is a journey through the history of Madrid, and, conscious of this, the chef admits that his job here is, in a certain way, to pamper the heritage of the Ritz by providing contemporary value. Influenced by French cooking, he knows by heart Auguste Escoffier's recipes—the foundation of modern cuisine—and hotelier César Ritz's traditions, but Dacosta is equally sensitive to local ingredients that have found their way into gastronomic pantries. Thus, when people leave Madrid, he wants them to take away with them not just the sights and nightlife but the unique flavors of this city—potato omelets, patatas bravas, squid bocadillos, croquettes—all with his delicate contemporary touch. If Escoffier was the grand ambassador of French cuisine, Dacosta has become one of the best ambassadors of Spanish culture and haute cuisine. The Ritz, located in front of the Prado Museum, and Dacosta's kitchens form an exceptional team: a unique merger of the arts and food.

The luxury Belle Époque–era Ritz is next to Madrid's famed "Golden Mile" of art, a one-kilometer stretch that is home to three of the best museums in the world: the Prado, the Thyssen-Bornemisza, and the Reina Sofía. This giant trio is located in the Paseo del Prado neighborhood and, together with Buen Retiro Park, was named to the UNESCO World Heritage list as a "Landscape of Light" on July 25, 2021. All of which has given the cultural landscape an exceptional universal appeal, defining it as a unique model of urbanism ahead of its time.

Paseo del Prado was the first of Europe's tree-lined urban promenades, starting when citizens began to use it as a place of recreation in the sixteenth century. In the late eighteenth century, during the reign of King Charles III, it turned into

Following pages: (left) Carlos Fitz-James Stuart y Martínez de Irujo, 19th Duke of Alba, photographed in the ballroom of his residence, Liria Palace. The Duke, together with the support of his two sons, has gone to great lengths to offer access to the House of Alba—from their palaces to their historic legacy. *(right) The White Duchess* is a life-size (192 x 128 cm) oil-on-canvas painting by the Spanish master Francisco Goya, completed in 1795. It portrays María Cayetana de Silva, 13th Duchess of Alba. It is one of the most celebrated artworks in the collection of the House of Alba, in Madrid's Liria Palace.

a model for other countries, giving rise to several notable projects on the other side of the Atlantic. This street is one of the most beloved aspects of the city. So much so that when a plan to cut down a grove of trees along the promenade to make way for a highway was proposed in 2006, Baroness Carmen Thyssen-Bornemisza did not hesitate to join the SOS Paseo del Prado platform and tie herself to a banana tree in front of her and her husband's Thyssen-Bornemisza Museum. "The trees are not going to be cut down! First they would have to cut off my arm," she said. This was a pivotal moment in the recent times of Madrid, and I particularly love these kinds of stories: citizens from all walks of life defending the city, adding to Madrid's raison d'être.

People in Madrid are authentic, and their alluring authenticity begins with prioritizing what is truly worthy in life. They do what they want because, as they say, "we do it the best." Being Madrileño is an attitude. Madrilenians walk, look, dress, and speak differently, with a genuine *castizo* cultural defiance. The *chotis*, the traditional folk dance of Madrid, is performed slowly, usually by taking three steps to the left, three to the right, and turning.

The thing is that Madrid has always moved to its own beat, and this goes along with its unique lifestyle and legendary late rhythm. Madrilenians seem to shape their entire schedules around social connections, turning meals into a center of gravity. Extraordinary proof of this is the enchanting *sobremesa*, a tradition so specific to Madrid that it doesn't seem to have a precise name in English. It is spending some leisure time after the meal, whether having a coffee or a digestif or simply chatting with your table companions, to relax.

Following pages: (left) "Flamenco is not just a dance, it is a way of life, an expression of the soul," says flamenco dancer and longtime Madrid resident Joaquín Cortés. *(right)* Celebrated flamenco singer Israel Fernández.

Relying on the magical power of shared moments, Marta Seco and Sandro Silva, owners of a gastro empire called Grupo Paraguas, have carried out an incredible culinary revolution that has changed not only the gastronomy but also the social life in the city. They started with a small Asturian cuisine restaurant named El Paraguas, after the square in Oviedo where they met, and have ended up with a large organization. Seco greatly appreciates the *sobremesa*, a concept that, in a way, proves that having lunch is an excuse to extend the encounter. She is a fanatical defender of what she calls "the encounter per se, our wonderful heritage," that is, gathering for the sake of it, not for drinking but for sharing and feeling life inexhaustibly. Having tapas at the high tables on Jorge Juan Street at their restaurant Ultramarinos Quintín, a store/dining room inspired by a traditional market, is the epitome of cool in Madrid. Quintín is one of their ten restaurants in the area, each with a different concept. Their success lies in the fact that they've managed to fill a gap in Madrid's gastronomy between high luxury and lower cuisine, creating restaurants with a classy, refreshing touch that Seco likes to brand as "the sophistication of authentic." The authentic, embodied by Madrid itself.

One can strongly feel the beating pulse of Madrid in the duo's restaurants around Jorge Juan, in the heart of the refined Salamanca neighborhood. They are places to connect not only with friends but also with friends of friends, and with people, maybe unknown, next to you. Seco and Silva love to provoke encounters in such a way that a gathering becomes a fiesta from two p.m. on; people laugh and hug, and the flowing energy of "all together" is extremely powerful, nothing short of electric.

People are aware of it, and they arrive as if they are going on a pilgrimage, proud of their socializing heritage. Very rarely does one go home right after work in Madrid. The energy that emerges after a day of hard work is the

best gift ever. Some like to call it simply *marcha*, a term meaning something that invigorates you and fills you with positive sensations. Maybe it's the sun, the light of the city, or the warmth of its people, or all those together, but you immediately want to be part of it. Seco and Silva's next project will convert the iconic architectural Metrópolis, dominating the Gran Vía, one of the main arteries, into a private club that is a gastronomy lifestyle destination, with international membership, a concept more and more popular in the city.

When people talk of Madrid's energy and how generous the city is, I always remember Javier Marías, an eminent Madrid writer and perennial candidate for the Nobel Prize, who passed away in 2022. He would praise this virtue of Madrid with a wonderful humorous touch: "People are so generous in Madrid that they even fight to pay the restaurant bills." And this is true. His intriguing and elegant novels were a flattering mirror of the cultivated class in impeccable locations, and effortlessly refined. Dinners at La Ancha, drinks at the Hispano, their houses in Almagro. Everybody wanted to live in the Madrid depicted by Marías.

Madrid's streets, parks, and buildings were immortalized in Ernest Hemingway's works. In his short story "The Denunciation," and in his only theatrical play, *The Fifth Column,* Hemingway talks about the Gran Vía and the legendary cocktail bar Chicote—supposedly Spain's first—which is still around, and which Spanish film director Luis Buñuel labeled "the Sistine Chapel of martinis." There, Hemingway created his own version of the daiquiri, the "Papa Doble," with rum, maraschino liqueur, pink grapefruit, and lemon…and lots of history. The Chicote bar is where Ava Gardner drank

Following pages: (left) Seventeenth-century Church of Saint Andrew the Apostle, one of the oldest churches in Madrid.
(right) Jeweler displaying designs on offer, including a multi-hued sapphire bracelet.

frozen gin and where, later, she and Frank Sinatra would mix with the most famous bullfighters of the day after attending her beloved bullfights at Madrid's Las Ventas Bullring, considered the most important in the world.

Ava Gardner spent twelve years living in Madrid, falling madly in love with the city, its traditions, corners, and people, who accepted her without questions. In a way, she had never really liked Hollywood. She did not fit in there, while in Madrid, she achieved her dream: becoming free.

Like the mythic Hollywood actress, Ernest Hemingway had a lifelong love affair with Madrid. The heavyweight of American literature visited Spain many times from the 1920s through the 1960s. He returned again and again to write, drink, visit the Prado, and watch bullfights, enjoying the fiestas and the nightlife and setting several short stories and novels here. He loved Paris and he lived in Cuba, but Madrid was the center of his world. In his novel *Death in the Afternoon,* he wrote, "When you get to know Madrid, it is the most Spanish of all cities, the best to live in, the finest people, month in and month out the finest climate....It is in Madrid only that you get the essence. The essence, when it is the essence, can be in a plain glass bottle and you need no fancy labels."

Hemingway understood, as few did, that Madrid's attraction was about its authentic people and about sharing real moments. No fuss. His fondness for the city made him turn it into "The Capital of the World," the same title the author gave to one of his renowned short stories, in which he revealed his infatuation with bullfighting and described Madrid as an "unbelievable place." Likewise, his passion for culture took him to the Prado Museum. His favorite painting was *Las Meninas,* Velázquez's portrait of King Philip IV's family. Time and time again, Hemingway was amazed by the effect this painting, one of the most important of Western art, had on him. All the figures are looking at the

viewer: the Infanta, her court servants, the queen's *meninas* (ladies-in-waiting), the dwarf, the king and queen reflected in a mirror in the background, a distant knight who enters the room, even Velázquez himself painting a large canvas. Everyone in the painting except Salomon, the sleepy Spanish mastiff dog, is looking outward. What a magical moment! This year marks the fortieth anniversary of its restoration, entrusted to British artist John Brealey, then head of restoration at the Metropolitan Museum of Art in New York. *Las Meninas* looks more splendid than ever. One of the most copied and imitated works in the history of art, *Las Meninas* has inspired sculptures of it in the streets of Madrid every autumn since 2018.

Countless artists and visitors have been enticed by the Prado Museum, but many others have also been seduced by Madrid's unbeatable combination of art scene and fiesta culture, just as Hemingway was. In the '90s, another giant, the British artist Francis Bacon, was charmed by the city and its late rhythm, its bars that emptied at dawn, its dry, baking heat and narrow, seamy streets. The pleasure derived from discovering the Spanish way of life was a tremendous gift to the artist, like a fresh source of energy. He loved the heat, he loved the food, he loved the pictures, and he was equally fascinated by the bullfight, or *corrida*, a motif that recurs in his work. Indeed, he described the *corrida* as "death in the sunlight" and "a marvelous aperitif to sex"!

However, it was at the Prado where Bacon spent rapt hours pondering the works of Goya and Velázquez, the artist who most influenced him. In his final years, Madrid became something of a haunt for Bacon, where he had an on-again, off-again relationship with a handsome young art-loving Madrilenian. They used to stop by the gentlemen's cocktail club Bar Cock to have a bottle of Krug and dry martinis at table nine, the couple's favorite. Bacon was always immaculately dressed, a perfect dandy, sitting with his back beautifully straight.

Everyone wants adventure in life, and Madrid, legendary for its party spirit, offers it in infinite quantities. In the '80s, Madrid's Movida Madrileña started to express a new freedom, especially at night, prompting the now-famous slogans *Madrid never sleeps* and *Madrid me mata* ("Madrid is killing me"). The latter phrase, a reference to the awesome nights of La Movida, was derived from designer Oscar Mariné's popular magazine *Madrid Me Mata*. Mariné's intention was to draft a love letter to Madrid, his hometown, and to its carefree, cocky, and witty spirit. The whole idea took root when he was in New York while his colleague and "guru," Milton Glaser, designed the "I ♥ NY" logo that became a legend. *Madrid Me Mata* continues springing back to life as if time has not passed.

The night has played a decisive role in the life of Madrid. Pedro Trapote, the famous impresario of Madrid nightlife and owner of some of its most mythic discos and other venues, proudly remembers the '80s, a time when the catchphrase was "Reinvent oneself or die" (very likely inspired by the Spanish philosopher Miguel de Unamuno). Something distinctive about Madrid is that it likes to face everything with a certain sense of adventure, perhaps a wonderful inheritance from Don Quixote. Like the adventurous protagonist in Cervantes's epic novel, Trapote left for New York in the mid-1970s and, after three days of waiting outside Studio 54, was finally let into the nightclub, which was once a Broadway theater. Returning to Spain, he placed an ad that read: "I buy a theater." That led to his acquisition of the Joy Eslava and Barceló theaters and the conversion of these temples of the night into a different concept: nightclubs. The most glamorous parties were held there during Madrid's heady Movida times, with Julio Iglesias, Tina Turner, and Stevie Wonder, to name a few, in attendance.

Following pages: (left) Elena Ochoa Foster photographed at the entrance to Ivorypress, a publishing house specializing in artists' books, which she founded in London in 1996. The Madrid outpost has an exhibition space and a bookshop.
(right) Convent of the Reparadoras, headquarters of the Supreme Council of the Inquisition at the end of the 1700s.

The nightlife of Madrid continues to be deeply fun and constantly reinventing itself. There's nothing better to energize oneself after an effervescent night than a delicious hot chocolate and churro around five or six a.m. The Chocolatería San Ginés, among the most emblematic sites in Madrid, is *the* place to enjoy the flour-based fried treat. Reminiscent of the cafés of the late nineteenth century, with traditional white marble tables and a counter covered in tiles, the chocolatería became the gathering point for national and international artists like Andy Warhol, Prince, Madonna, Pedro Almodóvar, flamenco legend Lola Flores, Diego Maradona, Naomi Campbell, Sting, and the Rolling Stones. Founded in the nineteenth century, it became famous when writer Ramón María del Valle-Inclán mentioned it in *Bohemian Lights,* a 1924 play that had his character Max Estrella touring magical Madrid during the last day of his life. Re-founded by Trapote in 1984, it has become a new symbol of Madrid throughout the world, with franchises in Tokyo, Shanghai, Miami, and Lisbon. The impresario still fondly recalls the visit of American president Jimmy Carter with his family, accompanied by an entourage of twenty people, expressly asking for "truncheons."

Madrid's nightlife—elevated to universal myth in Almodóvar's films, just as Woody Allen did for New York and Fellini for Rome—continues to be as intense and welcoming as ever. It simply accompanies you.

Very likely, Madrid's glamour emanates from its joie de vivre. In its heartfelt, lively, and energetic spirit, Madrid is effortlessly elegant. Somebody wrote that Spain's capital is like that impossibly chic aristocrat who is always regally dressed for dinner, no matter

Following pages: The home and gardens of a private collector. (*top left*) Bond II, a cast-iron sculpture by Antony Gormley, overlooks the pool.
(*top right*) The sculpture pavilion, with artworks by Louise Bourgeois, Alexander Calder, Germaine Richier, Antony Gormley, and Anish Kapoor.

what sacrifices are necessary for it. Whether or not this is so, Madrid chic is understated simply because its spirit is tremendously genuine. Authentic. Its subtle elegance with decorum, which comes from afar, has only matured with the passing of centuries. This becomes easy to understand when entering historian and interior designer Lorenzo Castillo's home, an eighteenth-century palace by Ventura Rodríguez, who, together with Juan de Villanueva, is considered the main architect of Madrid. In the heart of the historic district, the house took Castillo decades to furnish, mixing Spanish art from the sixteenth and seventeenth centuries with contemporary art, Louis XV furniture with art deco armchairs. Here we understand Madrid spirit, that in every era there is something fascinating, and that Madrid is a city composed of many cities, where everything comes together in a wonderfully authentic way. Houses, he feels, like cities, "must have a soul." His blend of the antique and modern is like Madrid itself, full of contrasts and surprises, enriching one another.

Castillo's projects have spanned all continents, including the Château Cheval Blanc of LVMH CEO Bernard Arnault in Bordeaux. He is known to spend years sourcing just the right piece. In an extraordinary manner, Madrid's style reflects one of his top rules of interior design: Concentrate on a few things of excellent quality, and with spirit and soul. Lunching at his home with his longtime friends Blanca Suárez; María Fitz James, countess of Jafarache; and Macarena Rey, he expresses his fascination with Madrid's ability to drink in the splendor of its past and find it with the present.

Many share this vision that Madrid has always been cool and powerful, since the time of the grand Habsburg monarchy and the Spanish Empire, especially from the heritage left by King Philip II. Castillo admires the "severe style" of this king, who was fond of Flemish architecture, with its redbrick walls and black-slate

roofs. This mirrored the austerity of Philip's dress, as depicted in portraits by Sánchez Coello, in which the king is dressed in a black doublet (black was the most expensive dye), a golden fleece his only ornament.

While we drink coffee, the conversation with Castillo and his friends turns to the two master painters whose imprint epitomizes Madrid's spirit: Velázquez and Goya. Diego Velázquez, the genius from Seville, became great at the court of Madrid, where he changed the colors of his palette from ochres and earth tones to black, silver, dry greens, and stained whites, a palette that Goya would later expand to pinks and pastels. Goya's grand art, regarded as a precursor to modern painting, is at the same time associated with the traditional spirit of Madrid, *el casticismo madrileño,* as the *majo* and *maja* types portrayed in his paintings were the iconic figures in Madrid traditional society during the eighteenth and nineteenth centuries. Elegantly dressed in a very elaborate style, with exquisitely embroidered *chaquetillas* (short jackets), they had a cheeky attitude that reflected the authenticity and indomitable free spirit of a city that continues to dazzle today in the twenty-first-century version of the *majo,* the *chulapo.*

There is a pop song that perfectly sums up the spirit of the city: "Vente pa Madrid" ("Come to Madrid"). It is an unabashed love letter that singer Antonio Carmona wrote in 1995 with his band Ketama, a new-flamenco fusion group at the time that has since disbanded.

This song is frequently heard on the grand patio of Castillo's house because Carmona along with his wife, Mariola Orellana, and his family are regulars at the designer's famous parties—a mix of aristocrats, writers, bullfighters, and

Following pages: (left) Details of the main staircase at the Norman Foster Foundation, located in Madrid's Chamberí neighborhood.
The headquarters are housed in a heritage-listed palace designed by Joaquín Saldaña López in 1912 for the Duke of Plasencia.
(right) Illustrating a resonance with Foster's architecture, a Ventus 2c glider, designed by Klaus Holighaus, hangs from the atrium.

flamenco singers—so reminiscent of those legendary times when Hemingway would celebrate with others in similar gatherings with one clear purpose: the enjoyment of life. In 2019, the song was rereleased in a new version. For the reissue, Ketama collaborated with Jorge Drexler, a Madrid native of Uruguayan origin, to include additional lyrics that movingly read:

*«Todos los martes son viernes
cuando te besa en los labios
esta ciudad que no duerme.
Y ser un recién llegado,
siguiendo el hambre de sueños,
yo he nacido en otro lado,
por tanto soy madrileño.»*

*"Every Tuesday is Friday
when it kisses you on the lips
this city that does not sleep.
And being a newcomer,
following the hunger for dreams,
I was born somewhere else,
therefore I am from Madrid."*

" I was extremely lucky to arrive in Madrid at the end of the '70s and be part of the Movida movement, the opening of Spain to the world. It was impossible not to get carried away by the frenetic pace of a city that never slept, and its inexhaustible flow of ideas and stimuli. The streets vibrated, and there, the most classic merged with the avant-garde in a perfect symbiosis. In that warm, colorful Madrid, where everything seemed possible, I met Carmen [Echevarria], the inspiration of my life and driving force behind my entire fashion project. She was passionately dancing at the legendary Cerebro nightclub while I, leaning on a column, watched her until our gazes met. It was a magical moment, those one-of-a-kind that only Madrid offers. Madrid will always be my muse. "

Roberto Torretta, *fashion designer*

❝ Madrid always awakens from its necessary siesta, which might explain why it never claims to be a city that never sleeps. Every hour, new dreams are born—relaxed on terraces, in charming markets, in bookstores with knowledgeable booksellers, or in the numerous cultural spaces hosting daily masterful encounters. Madrid's neighborhoods exude a beauty that captivates both longtime residents and newcomers. The city seamlessly blends its elements; this fusion is its art. This city is perfect just as it is. ❞

Paula Quinteros, *CEO, The Objective Media*

De M
al

*adrid
cielo*

> I am from Barcelona, and I have lived in many cities in the world, but Madrid fascinates me. It is a happy, open, and above all very authentic city, with its unique *castizo*, defiant spirit! In the effervescence that Madrid has experienced in recent years, UNESCO finally recognized [in 2021] the Landscape of Light as a World Heritage Site. An area that treasures the Golden Kilometer of art with three first-class museums: El Prado, the Thyssen, and the Reina Sofía, plus the entire Prado promenade and the Buen Retiro park. This recognition made me very happy because it could only happen in Madrid, and on top, it united beautifully two of my loves: art and nature. I love people in Madrid always striving to make the city better and better.

Baroness Carmen Thyssen-Bornemisza, *president of the Carmen Thyssen Málaga and Carmen Thyssen Andorra museums; vice president of the Thyssen-Bornemisza Collection Foundation, Madrid*

❝ When you get to know Madrid, it is the most Spanish of all cities, the best to live in, the finest people, month in and month out the finest climate. ❞

Ernest Hemingway, Death in the Afternoon

> Madrid has that wonderful quality, that it is constantly giving you something new, unexpected, and exceptional. You just have to take it. One of my cheeriest impressions was the installation of the twelve-meter white sculpture by Jaume Plensa, titled *Julia,* the bust of a young woman with her eyes closed at the Plaza de Colón in the core of the city. It will be there many more years, and looking at her, it becomes a moment of personal and intimate reflection, like if she was telling me, 'Slow down,' within the daily hectic dynamism.

Esther Alcocer Koplowitz, *Marchioness de Casa Peñalver and president of Grupo FCC*

Junio 2024

Dear vert,

MADRID-CHIC es un libro que edita ASSOULINE (NY) escrito por CRISTINA CARRILLO DE ALBORNOZ y –igual que con los ya editados de PARÍS, LONDRES y NUEVA YORK– pretenden contar y enseñar el momento actual de la vida de la ciudad.

Me han pedido mi casa y con ese motivo organizo un ALMUERZO (el Miércoles 12 de Junio) de amigos queridos, interesantes y (supongo) por supuesto muy Madrileños S. XXI.

Os necesito, y el libro de MADRID también!

Un abrazo,
Pablo

ALMUERZO
A las 2h

❝ One very interesting thing about the new Madrid is that it has understood that, to preserve the best, it has to renovate, add, and update. The best artisanship with artistic ambition—as we believe in Loewe—does the same. I am talking, for example, about turning the highway that surrounded the center into a seven-kilometer park, and buildings like the Sabatini hospital into the Reina Sofía, the great contemporary-art museum where *Guernica* is located. It's about keeping the best of the city and giving it new life. ❞

Sheila Loewe, *president, the Loewe Foundation*

❝ My life and my films are linked to Madrid like two sides of the same coin. Madrid is a city where you can be yourself, no matter how you are, and realize yourself as a person. It is the city of freedom. I am interested in the beautiful and spectacular part of Madrid, but also in the Madrid which is not so beautiful but is full of life and, above all, has an expressive force. In my films, I re-create an impossible Madrid, and it is rather amusing. An empty Plaza Mayor square like a de Chirico painting, or the main artery of Gran Vía, full of life, with all types of Madrid that fascinate me. In reality, in my films, more than a city, Madrid becomes something alive, a character that has its own life and changes. ❞

Pedro Almodóvar, *film director (who received the title of Adopted Son from the Madrid City Hall in 2018)*

1 Rafael García Garrido, general director of Nautalia Viajes and director of Las Ventas Bullring, the most important in the world. 2 Filiberto and Silverio Carrillo de Albornoz with friends at Teatro Barceló, the iconic theater turned nightclub. As Jorge Luis Borges wrote, "We live discovering and forgetting that sweet custom of the night." 3 Carmen Alcocer Koplowitz, Countess of Peñalver, consejera of Grupo FCC and Cementos Portland, on her terrace at home in Madrid. 4 Lulu Figueroa Domecq, one of the most celebrated young artists in Madrid, painting in her studio. Daughter of an aristocrat and the famous Domecq winery family, she has become a sophisticated fashion influencer as well. 5 Alicia Alcocer Koplowitz, president of Cementos Portland Valderrivas and consejera for Grupo FCC, in the Madrid mountains at La Sierra de Manzanares El Real with Ali, a rescued mare. Alicia is an honorary member of the National Association of Friends of Animals (ANAA) and the Animal Protection Foundation (FAADA). 6 Dinner at Esther Koplowitz's home in honor of Martine and Prosper Assouline. Esther, seated at center, is one of the most welcoming women in the city; her joyful, enthusiastic gatherings with people from different corners of the world bring the same magic that we feel in the city of Madrid. 7 Sassa de Osma, Princess of Hanover, at her Madrid home. Born in Lima, Peru, in 1988, and married in 2017 to Christian Hanover, she is a style icon and successful businesswoman as an ambassador for Dior. She is also Jorge Vázquez's right hand at the fashion brand Philippa 1970.

> Madrid cuisine has been evolving at the speed of a space rocket, but in this contemporary journey I never forget to pamper the local heritage, too. Entering the Ritz is a journey through the history of Madrid, and with D [Deessa, Dacosta's restaurant], when people leave Madrid, I want them to take away not just the sights and nightlife but the unique flavors of this city. My dream, since I have a room at the Ritz, which is in front of the Prado Museum, is to go to the Prado for an hour every day and study a painting.

Quique Dacosta, *Michelin-star chef*

" Madrid is like one of those wise teachers whispering secrets to celebrate life, dream, and love. Without this wonderful city, many of us would never have been who we became. I grew up sharing the feeling of great freedom with friends like Pedro Almodóvar and Andy Warhol, whom I remember fascinated by the creative explosion of Madrid in the '80s. The creativity is today at its best. Art flows in spurts from every corner, museums, institutions full of secrets, offering the best art to the world, and nonstop events such as the international prestigious annual ARCO Contemporary Art Fair. However, what moves me down to my heart is that Madrid is a museum of life; perhaps its greatest art is that it knows how to live. "

Jose Miguel, Viscount of Torre Hidalgo,
writer and co-founder of Magna Art Auctions

> **I can't imagine a greater gift for those who love history and literature. The streets and corners of Madrid are open pages, where you can read its rich past from the vital perspective of the city's vibrant present.**

Jaime Olmedo Ramos, *COO (technical director),*
Real Academia de la Historia

> **Life made me travel to the most distant places in the world before arriving at what should have been my starting point: Madrid, and Spain.**

Pablo Neruda, *writer and Nobel Prize winner*

> The city of Madrid is extraordinary. It has a human scale; in this sense it is an 'easy,' accessible city. Wonderfully intimate. However, what I find most satisfying is that in Madrid history is alive. A city that talks with the past and respects it. The city of Madrid, it has a large debt to architects such as Juan Villanueva. Not because he was responsible for beautiful buildings—although I do consider his original Prado Museum to be one of the nicest nineteenth-century buildings in Europe—but rather [there is] a certain feeling in the models he established, in proportional elements, the manner of putting brick and stone together. There is a certain manner that his colleagues learned from him; a sense of dignity and contention, which is very much down to Villanueva.

Rafael Moneo, *Pritzker Prize–winning architect*

An interview with Lady Foster of Thames Bank, founder and CEO of Ivorypress

What do you like most about living in Madrid?

Madrid is a city to walk and get lost in. I walk and walk and walk. Whether it's hot or cold, rain or shine…although the sky is almost always tinted in a transparent blue. I always discover a different shop, a florist with seasonal wildflowers, or a terrace that has suddenly emerged in a tiny square full of acacia trees. Nevertheless, there is a rule that I follow: before starting my walk, I go to La Duquesita and drink a hot coffee and a glass of water— always while standing.

What restaurants and dishes would you recommend in Madrid?

It's worth stopping by Taberna Verdejo to try one of the dishes on its menu that changes daily, and have some *pinchos* at the San Miguel Market and a beer at Cervecería Santa Bárbara. Dining on the fish of the day at Bistronómika or some sardines at El Pescador, eat a *cacio e pepe* in the Numa garden, a prawn salad at La Parra, and breakfast at the Hotel Santo Mauro. The list of restaurants and hotels in Madrid is endless.

What interests you most about Madrid? What surprises you?

The hubs and movements of artists belonging to a new generation who live in Móstoles and Carabanchel, neighborhoods of Madrid that have become artistic reference points, radically revolutionary. Because Madrid is always in constant and continuous reinvention, I feel that time is more elastic in Madrid than in other cities. You live very intensely, and it's really stimulating.

Do you think of Madrid as a cosmopolitan city?

Madrid is a provincial city by nature, and that is where its charm lies. And it remains provincial despite its cosmopolitanism. The global Madrid of these years continues to be intrinsically local. Despite recent developments and urban expansion, despite the new hotels and business openings…Madrid continues to be the same Madrid.

What is the new spirit of Madrid?

Madrid retains its usual charm. The same one I remember from my adolescence. It has evolved intelligently, welcoming everyone who has wanted to join its communities… Madrid is already a dream city, but dreams can fade. Moreover, those of us who love Madrid are here to ensure that it does not happen.

Madrid is legendary for its party spirit and celebration of life. How do you like to celebrate?

Going to the *zarzuelas* (Spanish opera) on Jovellanos Street. Walking through the Plaza Mayor and sitting down to have an aperitif before eating some fried eggs at Casa Lucio. The book fair on Paseo de la Castellana or any Sunday spent wandering on Cuesta de Moyano looking for a book. Signing up for a concert in the Plaza de Oriente or a bullfight at Las Ventas during San Isidro festivities. And if you prefer to feel calm one afternoon, there are the Royal Botanic Gardens right in front of the Prado Museum, or the terrace garden of the Juan March Foundation, my favorite place to disconnect, which is surprisingly located in the center of the city.

How would you define the elegance of Madrid?

The intrinsic elegance of our Madrid is the result of its friendly people. It is part of its idiosyncrasy. Of its humble corners with small anonymous shops lost in almost nameless neighborhoods, and the advertisements on the facades, designs worthy of a Pritzker Prize.

❝ In Madrid one can live very well with relatively little. The marvelous thing is we understand that luxury can be a simple moment of excellence. It is about savoir faire, like having with a friend the best *pincho de tortilla de patata* with a good wine. ❞

Xandra Falcó, *Marquise de Mirabel, president of Group Círculo Fortuny, and wine producer*

" I love that Madrid is a city of open streets, except for the old areas of the Austria-Habsburg period, allowing its wonderful light to penetrate in, and flooding joy. The light of Madrid invigorates me; it's like having a double-espresso coffee each time I step out! "

Diego Gronda, *co-founder and creative director, Gronda architecture*

> Every time you get out of your house, the city of Madrid exclaims: THANK YOU! I came to the generous Madrid, like so many, from Venezuela, and the city welcomed us with arms opened. At every corner, Madrid offers a heartwarming anecdote that reconnects us with our common history. Madrid gives us the gift of reunion, its blue sky bringing us closer to the tropics. I can't help but respond back with my eternal gratitude.

Ambassador Isadora Zubillaga,
Venezuelan ambassador to France

❝ I have always thought that Madrid is one of those cities that have a surprise around every corner. When I arrived here, back in 1965, I was amazed to see that there were two very different Madrids. A daytime, laborious, black-and-white one in which everything was a sin, and people worked from dawn to dusk. But when the sun set, another Madrid was born, that of the party animal, the crazy one, the one who never slept. It was the Madrid of the *tablaos,* of the marquises, of the partygoers. Almost sixty years later, Madrid continues surprising me. Now there are not only two Madrids but hundreds coexisting in it. The traditional Madrid has merged with us, Madrid residents born in different parts of the globe. Foreigners who, from the day they arrived here, feel part of this city that belongs to everyone. ❞

Carmen Posadas, *writer*

JAMES STEWART

ROMI SCHNEIDER

RITA HAYWORTH

FABIOLA DE BELGICA

S.A.R. DON JUAN CARLOS I

CAPTIONS

The 'High-Rise' Archive Gallery at the Norman Foster Foundation celebrates Norman Foster's radical approach to some of his most visible works: skyscrapers. Rather than following any established typology, these models, of both built and unrealized projects, explore the possibilities for creating a sustainable and inspiring vertical workplace.

Left: A caryatid sculpture on the facade of the Cervantes Institute headquarters in Madrid. Known simply as the "Caryatid Building," it is located on the elegant Alcalá Street.

Right: Mayor José Luis Martínez-Almeida on the rooftop of the city hall, located in the iconic Palacio Cibeles. He is one of the driving forces behind Madrid's success today.

Left: Things done well never go out of style, says Elisabeth Horcher, CEO of Horcher. A member of the fourth generation to run the legendary eighty-year-old restaurant, she is photographed at Buen Retiro Park.

Right: The Monument to Alfonso XII on the banks of the Estanque Grande del Buen Retiro, a huge artificial pond located in Buen Retiro Park.

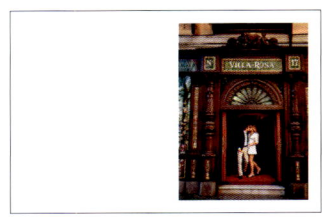

Painter Sandra Rojo Picón and her husband, Gabriel Suárez, cocreator of *Lucha de Gigantes*, a revolution of the contemporary art scene. They are photographed at Villa Rosa, a traditional establishment turned flamenco tablao; its facade is decorated with tiles by Seville artist Alfonso Romero Mesa.

Museo Nacional del Prado houses some of the finest works by Francisco Goya. These scenes are part of his well-known tapestry cartoons, paintings done in the late eighteenth century depicting everyday life in Madrid. They were designed for the Royal Tapestry Factory of Santa Bárbara near Madrid.

Left: Detail of a wounded horse and bird's wing from *Guernica* (1937), one of Pablo Picasso's most celebrated paintings, housed at the Reina Sofía Museum.

Right: Detail of the emblematic granite and brass Kilometer Zero plaque, in the Puerta del Sol. It marks the origin of the six national highways that depart from Madrid.

Family-run boutique hotel Hostal La Macarena, adjacent to the Plaza Mayor.

The living room of Sara Aznar and Nacho Ventosa, one of the most creative couples in Madrid. Their artistic and stylish home is in the boho-chic neighborhood of Las Salesas, presided over by an engraving by artist Eduardo Chillida. Owners of Los 33, the trendiest restaurant in Madrid, as well as El Viajero, they also have an events company called Cuatro Cuartos.

Left: Sisters Marta and Belén Ordovás Lladó have taken Madrid's creative scene by storm. The former is a designer, while the latter is an artist.

Right: Mayda Ybarra and her friend Xandra Falcó, Marquise de Mirabel, at the Frutas Vázquez, one of the finest fruit shops in the city. The two usually visit the frutería after shopping across the street at Mantequerías Bravo, a gourmet icon.

Left: The window of Oteyza, a boutique and workshop specializing in men's fashions.

Right: At the Mandarin Oriental Ritz hotel, a golden initial tops the main entrance doors. The hotel, a luxury retreat in Madrid, reopened in 2021 after three years of renovation.

Sandra Rojo Picón, one of the city's most talented young painters, puts the final touches on one of her iconic paintings representing dialogue with works by other modern painters. This one depicts a conversation with Jeff Koons's celebrated balloon dog.

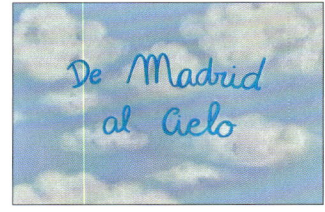

De Madrid al Cielo (2024), an oil painting by Sandra Rojo Picón completed especially for this book. Picón has created an immediately recognizable body of work, with clouds as a frequently recurring element. In this painting, clouds provide the backdrop for the popular saying *De Madrid al cielo* ("From Madrid to heaven").

Baroness Thyssen-Bornemisza at her home in La Moraleja, in front of a painting by Mercedes Lasarte. Born Carmen Cervera, the Baroness has received, among other honors, the Spanish Patron Award of 2018 and the Grand Cross of Isabel la Católica. She has also been recognized for her decisive efforts to bring the art collection of her husband, Baron Thyssen-Bornemisza, to Madrid.

Left: The official residence of the royal family, the Royal Palace is today used mostly for state ceremonies; when not in use, it is open to the public for tours.

Right: Fernando Fitz-James Stuart and Sofía Palazuelo Barroso, the Duke and Duchess of Huéscar. They are photographed in the gardens of Liria Palace, with their dachshund, Rumba.

Left: In the Santo Mauro Hotel's majestic Salón Rojo (Red Room). Formerly the ballroom of the Palace of the Duke of Santo Mauro, it was the epicenter of aristocratic society in the nineteenth century. In 1991, it opened as a hotel, which was fully renovated in 2022.

Right: Paula Quinteros, CEO of *The Objective*, an independent digital newspaper, at her Club Matador.

Left: One of Europe's greenest cities, Madrid has over forty major parks and many more smaller oases of calm.

Right: View of the facade of Madrid's CaixaForum art center, converted by Swiss architecture firm Herzog & de Meuron from an 1899 power plant. The art center is a new architectural point of interest that rises over old Madrid.

José Manuel Melgar, a close friend of the house, enjoying lunch at El Paraguas, the first restaurant of Grupo Paraguas, owned by Marta Seco and Sandro Silva. Seco and Silva just opened their tenth restaurant, The Library, an exclusive wine bar and boutique featuring Spain's most select wine club.

From cured meats to churros, Madrid boasts some of the greatest culinary offerings in the world. Top establishments in the city, whether for fine dining or casual bites, include OSA, Chocolatería San Ginés, Horcher, Lhardy, and Mantequerías Bravo, to name a few.

The kitchen at OSA, a Michelin-starred restaurant offering a one-of-a-kind dining experience featuring homemade cured meats, offal dishes, fish, and game. OSA is located near the banks of the Manzanares River, in a two-story chalet renovated by architect Jesus Colao that seats a total of twenty guests.

Left: Dinorah Alcock, owner of the restaurant OSA, hosted a dinner there organized with Ambassador Isadora Zubillaga. Other guests included writer Boris Izaguirre and his husband, Rubén Nogueira.

Right: Alejandra Ansón and Miguel Bonet, in the background, attending the dinner party at OSA.

Silhouette of one of the more than 200 active churches in the city.

Left: Taberna de la Elisa hand-painted wall mural, as traditional as the eatery's menu of Spanish tapas and dishes.

Right: The Metrópolis Building. Formerly an insurance company headquarters, it will be turned into a social, cultural, and gastronomic destination, including an international private club, by Grupo Paraguas.

Esther Alcocer Koplowitz, Marchioness de Casa Peñalver and president of Grupo FCC, in her garden with Harald, her Welsh springer spaniel.

Left: *Totem*, a stainless steel sculpture by Ellsworth Kelly, in the garden of a notable art collector.

Right: *Blade Runner*, a Richard Serra sculpture commissioned for the garden of a well-known art collector.

Left: The Palacio de Cristal ("Glass Palace"), a nineteenth-century conservatory located in Buen Retiro Park, currently used for art exhibitions. Built in the shape of a Greek cross, it is made almost entirely of glass.

Right: Retiro Park, opened to the public in 1868, was once part of the royal family's secondary residence.

Left: Jaime de Marichalar on the balcony of the assembly hall in the Real Academia de Bellas Artes de San Fernando.

Right: Museum cultural center Real Academia de Bellas Artes de San Fernando, housed in the eighteenth-century Goyeneche Palace.

Pascua Ortega, interior designer and intrepid host, organized a who's who of guests at his home. The nineteenth-century palace lies in the heart of the Literary Quarter, one of Madrid's most emblematic areas. "From Madrid to heaven. And for those who get bored of heaven, back to Madrid!" Ortega sent a handwritten note (*right, top left*) to guests inviting them to celebrate the making of the *Madrid Chic* book.

Pascua Ortega opened his home to host numerous guests including florist Inés Urquijo; Enrique Cambón; the Countess of Carvajal; interior designer Tomás Alía; fashion designer Roberto Torretta and his wife, Carmen Echevarria; antique dealer Alfonso Icaza; Katia Guerrero; model Mar Flores; and interior designer Belén Domecq.

Left: Madrid's glamour emanates from its joie de vivre, says Filiberto Carrillo de Albornoz, here at the entrance of the Santo Mauro Hotel with Laura Simón.

Right: Filiberto Carrillo de Albornoz and Laura Simón at the Santo Mauro Hotel's Gin Bar, a destination for signature cocktails.

Left: El Rastro flea market on Sundays and public holidays draws more than a thousand merchants.

Right: A vintage find at El Rastro flea market.

Seasonal arrangements at flower shop Dandelion, in the Salesas neighborhood.

Lorenzo Castillo hosts friends at his home, with a special appearance by Tana, his dachshund. Maria Fitz James Stuart, Viscountess of Jarafe, is CEO of Pelonio communications company. Blanca Suelves Figueroa, daughter of the Marquis of Tamarit, was the it girl of the nineties, and is still a reference in style. Macarena del Rey, producer of successful programs such as *Masterchef* and *Maestros de la costura* (Couture masters).

Left: Dentil molding adds a decorative flourish to a stately interior.

Right: Stone facades on the Centro District's elegant Calle de Fomento.

The visual appeal of Madrid's vibrant urban landscape takes many forms.

Left: Treasure hunting at El Rastro flea market.

Right: Dozens of booths are devoted to ephemera at El Rastro.

Left: Photographer Alberto García-Alix's Hasselblad camera, an indispensable tool of his trade.

Right: National Photography Award winner Alberto García-Alix, a leader in the 1980s countercultural Movida Madrileña movement.

Left: García-Alix's acclaimed photography portraits are not limited to people. Here, a feline subject.

Right: Motorcycles often crop up in García-Alix's work.

Left: The steel exterior of 85,000-seat Santiago Bernabéu Stadium, home to Real Madrid.

Right: The facade of the Four Seasons Hotel Madrid, once the headquarters of various banks.

A rooftop sculpture of chariots by Higinio de Basterra, crowning the former headquarters of the Bank of Bilbao and the current home of the Ministry of Environment.

Sheila Loewe is the great-granddaughter of Enrique Loewe Roessberg, founder of Loewe fashion house in Madrid in the 1800s. Sheila is the president of Loewe Foundation, whose Spanish poetry award, the Loewe Poetry Prize, has become a benchmark in the international cultural calendar.

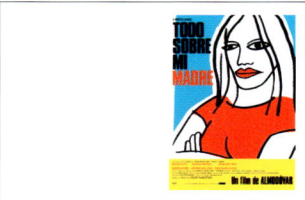

Mafalda Muñoz and Gonzalo Machado, superstar designers and owners of interior design studio Casa Muñoz and Gallery Machado-Muñoz, photographed at their home. Restored and decorated by the couple, it houses unique artwork, such as the ceiling sculpture by Aurèlia Muñoz.

Left: Carrara marble statue of the angel San Rafael on the facade of Almudena Cathedral, sculpted by Marco Augusto Dueñas.

Right: Carlos Galán founded Subterfuge Records, an independent record label, in 1989 in Spain.

The iconic poster for the Oscar-winning film by Pedro Almodóvar, *Todo sobre mi madre (All About My Mother)*, was designed by Spanish artist Oscar Mariné, born in Madrid in 1951.

Left: A woman in the Assouline corner at El Corte Inglés in Castellana in Madrid.

Right: The facade of El Corte Inglés on Serrano Street. This department store is a must-go destination in both Spain and Portugal for fashion, beauty, and first-class gourmet experiences and other outstanding services this chain has offered for more than eighty years.

Left: Sergio Simón at Club Deportivo Intacto practicing mixed martial arts.

Right: Laura Simón at a table at Café Gijón, possibly the most culturally significant café in Madrid. One can feel the presence of the great figures from the world of letters and arts who gathered at these tables.

Left: Cibeles Palace (Palacio de Cibeles), a fine example of the modernist architectural style, is a complex composed of two buildings.

Right: Mercedes Domecq, a master of the effortlessly chic look, started the decoration brand IQ Home with her sister Inés.

Clockwise, from top left: Rafael García Garrido; Filiberto and Silverio Carrillo de Albornoz; Carmen Alcocer Koplowitz, Countess of Peñalver; Lulu Figueroa Domecq; Alicia Alcocer Koplowitz; dinner at Esther Koplowitz's home; Sassa de Osma, Princess of Hanover.

Celebrated chef Quique Dacosta at his two-Michelin-star restaurant Deessa, the Mandarin Oriental Ritz hotel's signature restaurant. Located in the exquisite Alfonso XIII room, with a terrace overlooking the Ritz Garden, Deessa serves cuisine that is a gastronomic tale of sea and land—a story linked to the Mediterranean roots of the chef and Madrid.

Left: Marta Seco and Sandro Silva, owners of a gastro and lifestyle empire called Grupo Paraguas, have carried out a culinary revolution that has changed not only the gastronomy but also the social life in the city. They are photographed in front of Aarde, their restaurant next to the iconic Puerta de Alcalá monument.

Right: The 1911 neo-Renaissance Metropolis Building.

Left: Art Deco elegance in an apartment complex.

Right: Head of editorial content at *Condé Nast Traveler Spain*, David Moralejo, and editor Clara Laguna at *Condé Nast Traveler Spain*.

Multi-disciplinary artist Belén Ordovás Lladó at her studio.

The interior courtyard in Madrid's neoclassical National Archaeological Museum. Designed by architect Francisco Jareño, it opened in 1867 on the Plaza de Colón. The museum houses a unique collection spanning from prehistory to the early-modern age. One of the highlights is the Iberian stone sculpture of the Lady of Elche.

Unwinding during the popular pastime of botellón—gathering in the streets to socialize with a botella (bottle) in hand.

Left: Marta Ordovás Lladó indulges in some classic Madrid fare at Casa Macareno Tapas Restaurant.

Right: A no-frills bar serving wine and spirits is an essential stop on a visit to Madrid.

Hand-painted fans displayed as decorative art in a shop on the Plaza Mayor.

From the architecture and fine arts to the meticulously crafted lighting fixtures, the beauty of Madrid is in the details.

Artisan Javier Sanchez Medina at his Malasaña shop creates animal heads out of natural fibers based on centuries-old techniques.

Left: Pritzker Prize-winning architect Jean Nouvel recently completed an extension at the Reina Sofía Museum, Spain's national museum of twentieth-century art.

Right: City Hall, housed in Madrid's former main post office and telegraph and telephone headquarters, a building that dates back to 1919.

Left: Inside the atelier and boutique Oteyza, a menswear firm celebrated for its handcrafted shirts.

Right: Paul García, designer and co-owner of the menswear boutique and atelier Oteyza.

Left: Details of the nearly 170-year-old tavern Viva Madrid, with a facade tile featuring the Cibeles Fountain. Dating back to 1856, the venerable establishment is now a restaurant.

Right: Painter Sandra Rojo Picón and her husband, Gabriel, at a traditional tapas bar.

Mafalda Muñoz at her home in central Madrid, a mix of old- and new-world refinement restored and designed by her and her husband. The sofa and lamp are by their own firm, Interior Architecture Studio Casa Muñoz.

Left: Stylist, creative consultant, and *Harper's Bazaar* editor-at-large Beatriz Moreno de la Cova.

Right: A 2015 issue of fashion magazine *Harper's Bazaar Spain*. Pictured on the cover: models Blanca Padilla and José María Manzanares, photographed by Thomas Whiteside.

Left: Self-portrait by eighteenth century Spanish painter Luis Paret y Alcázar, at the Prado Museum.

Right: Las Meninas (1656), by Diego Velázquez, a masterwork of Western art at the Prado.

The Third of May 1808, by Francisco Goya, depicts the aftermath of the rebellion against the French occupation of Spain, 1814. Prado Museum.

Left: Lhardy, a luxury restaurant opened in 1837, is where Queen Isabella II would dine with friends to savor the Cocido madrileño, a traditional dish with a chickpea base.

Right: Mayda Ybarra and Xandra Falcó, Marquise de Mirabel, enjoy the traditional Cocido madrileño with a bottle of XF rosé at Lhardy.

Left: Miniaturist Carlos Díaz de Bustamante and his ever-present guitar.

Right: Microworlds in a box created by Díaz de Bustamante.

Left: Pedro Trapote and Begoña García-Vaquero, one of the most beloved couples in Madrid society. The king of Madrid nightlife, Trapote owns clubs such as Joy Eslava and Barceló in addition to the popular late-night snack shop, Chocolatería San Ginés, which earned an award from Madrid's City Hall.

Right: Pedro Trapote always has the best tickets for the corrida at Las Ventas.

Left: Pageantry and drama at Las Ventas Bullring.

Right: The Neo-Mudéjar entrance with hand-painted tiles at Las Ventas Bullring.

Writer and bullfighting entrepreneur Simón Casas, whose first bullfight with picadors took place at Las Ventas in 1967.

Two generations enjoying the sport, which originated in Spain nearly 300 years ago.

The third-largest bullring in the world, Las Ventas can seat 23,798 spectators.

Tío Pepe sherry sign on the Puerta del Sol, a beloved Madrid landmark.

Left: Madrid's Palacio Real, or Royal Palace, built on the site of a royal residence that was destroyed by fire in 1734.

Right: Cathedral of Saint Mary the Royal of the Almudena, dedicated to the patroness of the city, now serves as the seat of the Roman Archdiocese of Madrid.

Left: The Church of St. Genesius, one of the oldest houses of worship in the city, dates to 1645.

Right: Restaurateurs Sara Aznar and Nacho Ventosa at their wildly popular Los 33.

Left: The imposing nineteenth-century façade of the Bank of Spain, the central bank responsible for the country's monetary policy.

Right: The oldest hotel in Spain, the Petit Palace Posada del Peine near Puerta del Sol dates from 1610.

Left: The brick-and-stone exterior of the Church of San Andrés, on the site of an early Christian temple in Islamic Madrid.

Right: Amaia de Meñaka, founder of the We Collect gallery, which showcases emerging and established artists.

Left: Contemporary lines in a city steeped in architectural tradition.

Right: Plaza de Colón, named in honor of Christopher Columbus, features the twin Torres de Colón.

Left: Lighting that evokes the past…

Right: …and the future, here at luxury fashion house Loewe's flagship store.

Aerial view of the Supreme Court of Spain (foreground), once a convent, on the Plaza de la Villa de Paris.

A Sorolla painting, flanked by two Venetian figures from the seventeenth century, looms large in a room of Lorenzo del Castillo's home. The rug features a Chinoiserie design. The space brings together influences from around the globe.

Left: The grandeur of the Spanish monarchy on full display in a ceiling at Palacio Royal. Lining the walls of the palace are works by Caravaggio, Velázquez, Goya, and other Spanish masters.

Right: Home to the Duke of Alba—one of Spain's most aristocratic families—the Palacio de Liria is now open to the public.

Lorenzo del Castillo's home is a delight for the senses. A treasure trove of one-of-a-kind pieces combined with a keen eye for design, the rooms at the decorator's abode are a testament to his artistry. These rooms feature pieces by Maison Jansen and Willy Rizzo.

Left: The models and sculptures placed in the main staircase of the Norman Foster Foundation explore the resonance of the airplane for art and architecture. Pictured here is the Beijing Capital International Airport.

Right: More than just the capital of Spain, Madrid is also a capital of art, design, and fashion. This is seen in the homes of its inhabitants.

View of the Carrera de San Jerónimo and Paseo del Prado with a Procession of Carriages, Jan van Kessel III, 1686. This masterpiece is on display at the Museo Nacional Thyssen-Bornemisza, Madrid

Left: In the home of art dealer and curator Marta Ordovás Lladó.

Right: Ordovás Lladó, a champion of contemporary art, relaxes at home.

Left: Nino Redruello, co-owner and chef at Club Financiero, tastes monkfish in the kitchen prior to service. Redruello embodies something idiosyncratic in the people of Madrid: Never forget your roots.

Right: Javier S. Medina outside his shop Carpintería 28. The artisan uses only natural materials—rattan, raffia, and other fibers—in his popular creations.

Left: Exhibition at Sushita restaurant with acrylic and tempera paintings by artist Eugenia Martínez de Irujo, 12th Duchess of Montoro. Her joyful bird and flower motifs adorn the tableware and jugs.

Right: The Duchess and her husband, Narcís Rebollo, President of Universal Music Spain and Portugal, at Sushita.

The sumptuous Metropolis, built between 1907 and 1910, presides over the Gran Vía. In addition to its neo-Renaissance façade and dome with gold inlay, the building is topped with a statue of Winged Victory.

Left: Landmarked Biblioteca Nacional de España houses a vast collection of books, maps, manuscripts, and other ephemera.

Right: One of Madrid's many ornate wooden doors.

Left: Inside Colecciones Reales, the Royal Collections Gallery, which traces 500 years of history.

Right: Chef Javier Bonet of Sala de Despiece ("Cutting Room") offers a menu of barely cooked ingredients with a creative twist.

Left: Part clothing store, part art museum, Galería Comercial is a nextdoor extension of Sala de Despiece.

Right: In keeping with the Sala de Despiece concept, items at Galería Comercial are displayed as though they were food.

Lavish Mediterranean lunch at the exquisite Numa Pompilio, with its stunning secret garden.

Left: Nacho Ventosa at Los 33 restaurant. The Uruguayan-inspired cuisine and traditional music have made it a favorite in the city.

Right: The Birth of the Sun and the Triumph of Bacchus, ceiling fresco by Corrado Giaquinto, 1761, at the Royal Palace.

Opened in 2008, cultural center CaixaForum Madrid was designed by Swiss architects Herzog & de Meuron. The exterior is easily recognized of *The Vertical Garden* by Patrick Blanc.

Left: Architect Diego Gronda and his daughter Malena in his garden next to the reflecting pool. Gronda transformed this Francisco Cabrero-designed home into a twenty-first century construction. The renovation is an inspiration for Madrid's modern architecture scene.

Right: Neptune Fountain, in the Plaza de Cánovas del Castillo, is one of Madrid's most iconic monuments.

Monument to Alfonso XII on the lakeshore in Buen Retiro Park.

Enjoying the sunset in Retiro Park is a lovely end to a day in Madrid.

Young love in Retiro Park—a space to escape the bustle of the city.

Madrid's old-world charm is found in the quiet corners of the capital.

Left: Paula Quinteros, CEO of the newspaper *The Objective*, at Club Matador.

Right: A characteristically lavish interior in the Royal Palace.

The home of former Christie's Spain CEO Juan Várez and Dutch designer Jan Taminiau.

Left: The city is filled with gardens, parks and flower markets that add pops of color to the urban landscape.

Right: Effy Betancourt and Diego Mignot enjoy time together at home.

Left: Cibeles Fountain is synonymous with kings. Built in the eighteenth century by the order of King Carlos III, it now hosts the kings of Real Madrid Football Club for their victory parades.

Right: Isabel Díaz Ayuso, President of the Community of Madrid, in Puerta del Sol. One of the most popular politicians of the last decade, this woman has changed the city for the better.

Gonzalo Machado at his home in Madrid. Owner of interior-architecture studio Casa Muñoz and gallery Machado Muñoz with his wife Mafalda Muñoz, he is also a photographer. He sees Madrid as a wonderfully attractive woman with an overflowing, fun energy, and with whom you cannot help but fall in love.

  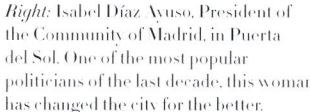  

Clockwise, from top left: Head Parque Norte, by Arturo Berned; *Julia*, by Jaume Plensa; Galería de las Colecciones Reales; Royal Basilica of St. Francis the Great; Museo Nacional del Prado; Biblioteca Nacional de España; Roy Lichtenstein sculpture at the Reina Sofía Museum; and *Monument to the Discovery of America*, by Joaquín Vaquero Turcios.

Rococo and neoclassical accents at the Royal Palace of Madrid.

Writer Carmen Posadas at her home. Author of more than thirty books and essays translated into more than twenty languages, she was awarded the Premio Planeta de Novela, one of the most important literary prizes in the Spanish language.

Left: Portrait of Napoleon III, a Gobelins tapestry, at Liria Palace.

Right: Everyday moments become works of art in the warm light of Madrid.

Left: Redbrick buildings frame the historic Plaza Mayor.

Right: Multi-disciplinary artist Rorro Berjano spotted in Madrid.

Left: Life in Madrid is like a painting in progress—full of possibility.

Right: A local dressed for the weather—with around 350 days of sunshine a year, Madrid is one of the sunniest capitals in Europe.

Left: Traditional tapas at Bodegas el Maño.

Right: With more than 15,000 bars, Madrid is known for its nightlife.

The dining scene doesn't begin in earnest until at least 8 p.m., in part due to late lunches and afternoon siestas.

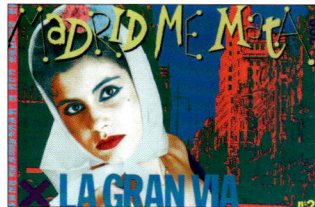   

Madrid Me Mata magazine was created by artist Oscar Mariné in the 1980s. The magazine was a love letter to the city. This cover features two great symbols of Madrid: the Gran Vía, one of the city's main arteries, and a woman dressed in true Madrid fashion.

Teatro Barceló is a cinema-theater turned-nightclub. In the 1980s, it was a club called Pacha and became the epicenter of the city's legendary nightlife, bringing together all the beautiful people: artists, politicians and aristocrats. The impresario Pedro Trapote, who acquired the space in 1996, continues its mythical legacy.

Left: Bar La Vía Láctea launched some of the biggest names in music during the 1980s countercultural Movida Madrileña.

Right: Artist and cultural influencer Fatima de Burnay relaxes over a drink with author Ray Loriga at Museo Chicote, a cocktail bar in Madrid.

Photos of celebrity patrons bedeck the walls at Museo Chicote, an Art Deco bar that's been open for business since 1931.

Left: Neon red lights and velvet curtains at alt-music nightclub Club Malasaña.

Right: Anything goes at Club Malasaña. Laura Vandall, mastermind of the club, is pictured top left. Madrid's nightlife is for friends, dancers, lovers, and anyone looking for some quintessential Spanish passion.

Left: Taking a break from the dance floor at La Discoteca.

Right: Signage for La Discoteca, one of the more upscale dance clubs in town.

Techno rhythms and pulsating house beats keep clubbers going until dawn.

Aerial view of Madrid, a city where, in the words of Federico García Lorca, "every corner has a story to tell."

AUTHOR'S ACKNOWLEDGMENTS

This is my seventh book with the extraordinary Assouline publishing house. I am grateful as ever to my publishers, Martine and Prosper Assouline, for realizing that it was the right moment to do a book about Madrid. This time my recognition goes beyond their trust in me. Making this challenging book with them, and Martine in particular, has been a unique life lesson, realizing, as madrileños do, what is truly worthy in life. This alone is simply invaluable.

Cheers to the talented artist photographer Oliver Pilcher. A gift to work together.

In order to capture the beating spirit of Madrid, I tried to follow its frenetic, joyful and artistic rhythm. Most importantly, I was led, welcomed, and supported by precious friends and friends of friends. This was the only way to make and write a real book about Madrid.

First of all, my greatest appreciation to the Duke of Alba and the Duke and Duchess of Huéscar for welcoming us at Liria Palace. Much obliged to Madrid mayor José María Almeida and President of La Comunidad de Madrid, Isabel Díaz Ayuso. I am full of heartfelt gratitude to dearest Esther Alcocer Koplowitz, Marchioness of Casa Peñalver; Begoña García-Vaquero; Ambassador Isadora Zubillaga; Lady Elena Ochoa Foster; and Eugenia Martinez de Irujo, Duchess of Montoro, and Narcis Rebollo. A special thanks to the marvelous Esther Koplowitz, Marchioness of Cárdenas, and to Alicia and Carmen Alcocer Koplowitz, countess of Peñalver.

A big thank you to Rafael Medina, Duke of Medinacelli, Mayda Ybarra and Xandra Falcó, Marquise of Mirabel, as well as to Baroness Carmen Thyssen-Bornemisza, for their constant support.

It was a privilege to have doors opened to the most magnificent houses of Pascua Ortega and Lorenzo del Castillo, and to the splendid residence and gardens of one of the best private collections in the world. I feel equally appreciative for Mafalda Muñoz and Gonzalo Machado, and Sara Aznar and Nacho Ventosa, and to Diego Gronda, for receiving us in their homes.

A big thank you to the painter Sandra Rojo for generously contributing the painting *De Madrid al Cielo*, and to her and Gabriel Suárez's tremendous support. And to Oscar Mariné for providing his genius designs. Equally to artist Lulu Figueroa Domecq and to architect-sculptor Arturo Berned.

A special thank you to architect Rafael Moneo, as well as to Jaime Olmedo and Carmen Posadas. Equally grateful to film director Pedro Almodóvar and his company El Deseo.

I would like to recognize Cristina Alvarez Guill, Paula Quinteros, Sheila Loewe, Roberto Torretta, and Carmen Echevarria. And to Sassa de Osma, Blanca Suelves, Macarena del Rey, and Maria Fitz James.

Thank you so much for the warm reception by Elisabeth Horcher, Marta Seco and Sandro Silva, Pedro Trapote, Nino Redruello, Dinorah Alcock, Quique Dacosta. Equally thankful to Lhardy, Sushita, Chocolatería San Ginés, Mantequerías Bravo, and OSA. And to the hotels: the Ritz, Four Seasons, and Santo Mauro (Alicia Catalán). My gratitude goes as well to Teatro Barceló and Pablo Trapote.

I wish to acknowledge profusely the museums: The Prado, The Thyssen-Bornemisza, and the Reina Sofía, as well as the Colecciones Reales. A special thanks to Jaime de Marichalar, who helped us in opening the doors of the Real Academia de Bellas Artes de San Fernando.

This endeavor would not have been possible without the Assouline team, mostly the senior editor Scout Sabo and the senior photo editor Andrea Ramírez Reyes.

I am beyond grateful to my husband, Emilio and my three sons—Emilio, Silverio, and Filiberto—for their endless encouragement, and assisting in the making of *Madrid Chic*. Massive thanks to all.

—Cristina Carrillo de Albornoz Fisac

PUBLISHER'S ACKNOWLEDGMENTS

The Publisher expresses their gratitude to all the wonderful madrileños who participated in this book, which included some very good friends, in particular Jaime de Marichalar, who led Prosper and Martine to discover and love Madrid.

PHOTOGRAPHER'S ACKNOWLEDGMENTS

I would like to dedicate this book to my family—Abigail, Andalucía, Bianca, Constantina, and Herb—who supported me throughout the making of this project.
—Oliver Pilcher

CREDITS

All Images © Oliver Pilcher, except: page 23: All Rights Reserved; pp. 76-77: © Sandra Rojo Picón, *De Madrid al Cielo*, Oil on Paper, 42 x 29, 7 cm; p. 78: Courtesy of Baroness Thyssen-Bornemisza; p. 89 (top left): © Stefano Politi Markovina/Alamy Stock Photo; pp. 104, 105: © Luis Mendoza Cruzado; p. 107 (top left): © Pascua Ortega; pp. 139, 278-279: © Oscar Mariné/www.oscarmarine.com; p. 147 (top left and bottom): © Carlos Neville; p. 262: (top left) Photo by Sergio Padura; (top right) © Andrea Comas, courtesy Ayuntamiento; (bottom right) © Reina Sofía Museum; p. 263: (top left) © Patrimonio Nacional.

Every possible effort has been made to identify and contact all rights holders and obtain their permission for work appearing in these pages. Any errors or omissions brought to the publisher's attention will be corrected in future editions.

Assouline supports *One Tree Planted* in its commitment to create a more sustainable world through reforestation.

Front cover: © Oliver Pilcher. Artwork: Juan Bauzil, *Carlos IV from Behind*, 1818. Oil on canvas, 28 x 21 cm. El Escorial, Casa de campo del Príncipe, National Heritage.
Back cover: © Oliver Pilcher.
Endpages: © Oliver Pilcher.

© 2024 Assouline Publishing
3 Park Avenue, 27th floor
New York, NY 10016 USA
Tel: 212-989-6769 Fax: 212-647-0005
assouline.com

Senior designer: Dylan Brackett
Senior editor: Scout Sabo
Senior photo editor: Andrea Ramírez Reyes

Printed in Italy by Grafiche Milani.
ISBN: 9781649804266

All rights reserved.
No part of this publication may be reproduced or transmitted in any form or by any means, electronic or otherwise, without prior consent of the publisher.